how to 'cook' compost

9 8 7 6 5 4 3 2 1
First published in 2008

Packaged by Susanna Geoghegan for
National Trust Books
10, Southcombe Street
London W14 0RA

An imprint of Anova Books Company Ltd

ISBN: 9781905400577

© Complete Editions
Printed in China by CT Printing

CONTENTS

INTRODUCTION

Over the centuries different civilisations have come to understand the value of making and using compost. And for most of this history making compost was a simple matter of having more to eat.

Applying compost to the land improved the soil, made plants healthier and produced better yields at harvest time.

The same holds true today. However, compost making has a further benefit now, which would never have concerned our ancestors. Faced with the grave environmental consequences of continuing to bury ever-growing volumes of organic waste in landfill sites, which in turn create harmful greenhouse gases as well as eating up land that could be put to better use, making compost provides a simple and rewarding means of recycling all but a tiny amount of the organic waste we produce.

Better still there is no cost attached, except, possibly, for buying a compost bin at the outset – although many of these are now available from local authority purchase schemes at significantly reduced prices, some as low as £3.

As you'll discover later on, however, you don't even need to have a bin to make compost. If you can lay your hands on a piece of old carpet or sacking, you can turn much of your kitchen and garden waste into compost quite satisfactorily.

If you want further inspiration, log on to the National Trust website (www.nationaltrust.org.uk) and discover the initiatives that the Trust has undertaken at many properties, including Cotehele, near Saltash on the Devon–Cornwall border. Here it has initiated an estate-wide project to reduce its carbon footprint by composting waste from the restaurant and tea-room as well as the homes of the sixty tenants who live at Cotehele.

Those tenants are recycling their kitchen and garden waste to make compost in the same way that we all can. There are various ways of doing this, as this book explains, but the principles behind them are the same and there has never been a better time to make a start and begin to appreciate the benefits that making compost provides.

As one author on the subject suggests (possibly tongue-in-cheek) in the title to his book, don't forget that when you have finished reading this one and have fully absorbed its contents, you can tear it up and put it on a compost heap.

Can there be a more striking way of literally putting words into action?

STARTER FOR TEN – ALL YOU NEED TO KNOW ABOUT COMPOST

- **What is compost?**

The compost you can make in your garden is produced from decayed organic matter. However, there are different kinds of composts available from garden centres and other suppliers. These combine 'garden' compost with other materials to produce particular composts for growing seedlings and plants in pots.

- **What is garden compost used for?**

Home-made garden compost is a soil conditioner: it improves the structure of soil; it acts as a fertiliser and it can also be used as a mulch to suppress weeds and retain moisture. Compost has the further benefit of recycling material that would otherwise have to be disposed of elsewhere – frequently in landfill sites.

- **What can be composted?**

This book clearly explains what garden materials and

household waste can be composted. A small number of
materials (particularly cat and dog faeces, cooked food,
meat, metal, glass and plastics) should not be added, but,
in the right proportions, a wide range of material from egg
boxes and tea bags to young hedge clippings and bedding
plants can be added to a compost heap.

• **What about special equipment?**
About the only essential piece of equipment you will need
to make compost is a garden fork. However, a compost bin
will keep the compost heap neater. These can be made at
home (following instructions such as those on pages
33–38); there are also many ready-made compost bins
available on the market. If you already have a garden
shredder, that can be helpful in breaking down woody
material before adding it to the compost heap, but there
is no need to buy a shredder in order to make compost.

• **Does making compost take a lot of time and work?**
As with most aspects of gardening, the more work you
put in to making compost, the greater the return. Once
you are set up to make compost, the process does not
need to take a great deal of effort. However, if you have

energy and the inclination you can opt to 'turn' a compost heap, which does speed up the composting process.

• How quickly will compost be ready for use?

Given the right conditions, it is possible to make compost inside twelve weeks. On the other hand it can also take as long as a year. It depends which method you opt for and how much time you spend working on your compost heap.

• Does compost attract vermin?

Provided you add appropriate ingredients, vermin will not be drawn to a compost heap any more than they are to other areas of the garden. If vermin, such as rats, are already present in the area, they may visit a compost heap, just as they may visit other parts of your garden. In either case remedial action can be taken to deal with them and any other unwanted visitors.

One solution is to bury wire netting 30cm deep in the ground all round your compost heap. That will deter rats. Another possibility is to buy one of the commercially produced compost bins that has a rat-proof base.

- ## Does compost spread weeds and plant diseases?

As above, provided that you stick to the right ingredients, the heat generated in a compost heap will kill weeds and diseases. Some weeds and the spores carrying certain plant diseases will survive the conditions in a cool compost heap and they should not be added if this is the process you plan to follow.

- ## Is heat essential in a compost heap?

Heat helps to make compost quicker and it does kill weeds and plant diseases with appropriate ingredients, but heat is not essential. If your compost heap is built up over a long period it may never get particularly hot. By the time it is ready for use though, the compost produced will be just as good as that produced in a heap that has reached higher temperatures.

- ## Is compost safe to touch?

Follow the usual hygiene precautions you use in the rest of the garden and compost will present no additional hazards. You should keep your anti-tetanus protection up to date. Cuts should be kept covered. And you should always wash your hands before eating.

WHAT'S THE POINT OF MAKING COMPOST?

Since composting is nature's own and oldest way of recycling waste and fertilising the soil, why not leave nature to get on with it?

Put simply, making compost is a 'win–win' process. It gives nature a helping hand by speeding up the breaking down and recycling of organic material. At the same time, if we make compost, our families and our gardens benefit. And by making compost at home, we make a small but valuable contribution to a national – in fact a global – movement to reduce the damaging disposal of waste.

If that sounds a bit extreme, here are some facts:

- Each year in the UK we produce more than 434 million tonnes of waste – and we do this at a rate that would fill the Albert Hall in London every two hours!
- In 2003–2004 72% of municipal waste in England was disposed of in landfill sites.
- The organic materials that end up in landfill sites are a major source of methane in England, and methane is a greenhouse gas twenty times more powerful than carbon dioxide.
- These organic materials also produce a liquid known as leachate. If this ever enters water supplies it can pollute them.
- Even incinerating waste does not dispose of it altogether. Almost 30% of the original mass is left over and has to be sent to landfill, while wasting resources in the process.

That's the dilemma we all face.

These are some of the measures being taken to deal with it:

- The UK government has set a target to recycle 40% of all household waste by 2010, rising to 45% by 2015 and to 50% by 2020. That means a big reduction in the amount of green and kitchen waste going into household bins.
- Another government target has established that by 2020 the amount of biodegradable municipal waste sent to landfill must be reduced to 75% of the amount produced in 1995.
- In addition to individuals recycling organic waste by making compost at home, community-wide schemes are being developed to undertake composting on a larger scale.
- According to DEFRA, 'As recently as 1998, 92% of municipal waste comprised green wastes collected from civic amenity sites or local authority parks and gardens, with only 7% of organic municipal wastes collected at the kerbside.'

Composting may be good for the wider community, but what's in it for individual households? In other words, is making compost worth even the small effort involved? If you can answer 'yes' to any of these questions, you have your answer.

- Would you like your dustbin to be lighter?

  (Removing waste for composting can reduce the contents of the average dustbin by more than a third.)

- Would you like to prevent smells coming from it?

  (Some organic materials can start to smell after a few days in the dustbin. Compost them and their smell is removed.)

- Would you like to save money on bought composting materials, mulches and fertilisers?

  (Making compost at home creates something valuable from waste materials – and it's free!)

- Would you like to improve the condition of the soil in your garden?

  (Compost opens up heavy clay soils, and retains moisture and nutrients in light and sandy soils.)

- Would you like to grow healthier plants that are less vulnerable to disease?

  (By recycling nutrients back into the soil, compost

promotes the health of your plants and helps to improve yields of fruit, vegetables and flowers.)

- Would you like to have more time to enjoy your garden by cutting down on weeding it?

(Compost is an ideal mulch to suppress weeds.)

- Would you like to save money on your water rates by watering your garden less?

(As a mulch, compost also helps retain moisture lost through evaporation, which means you don't need to water your plants as often.)

- Would you like to help preserve peat bogs by stopping the use of peat-based composts?

(Peat bogs have taken many thousands of years to develop. Stopping the extraction of peat from them is essential to help preserve them for the future.)

Maybe the question at the head of this section should be turned round to ask, 'What's the point of <u>not</u> making compost?'

WHAT CAN I DO WITH COMPOST?

Of course, simply deciding to make compost immediately presents you with one very significant benefit. As mentioned earlier, composting household and garden waste recycles a lot of organic material that would otherwise end up in landfill sites, with all the environmental consequences that lead from that.

However, compost obviously benefits the garden as well...

As a soil improver
Compost improves soil structure. When it is worked into heavy clay soils through the actions of worms, it helps break up the dense soil. This means that the soil will begin to drain more freely as well as more readily releasing plant nutrients locked inside it.

By contrast, the crumbly structure of compost benefits light sandy soils as well, where it helps them retain moisture and plant nutrients which would otherwise be washed away before the plants growing in the soil can benefit fully from feeding on them. Digging compost into the soil will immediately begin to help improve it.

As a plant food

Compost is rich in plant nutrients and mineral trace elements itself. Spread on the soil as a top dressing, it will release these slowly. If you apply compost in spring and summer your plants will be able to make the best use of it as a feed.

When you are planting new plants, dig in compost to give them a good start.

You should water the soil well before applying compost, or spread it after a fall of rain.

Different plants require different amounts of compost. The greatest recommended density is one wheelbarrow of compost to every five square metres of soil. This will suit plants like blackcurrants, brassicas, potatoes, roses and tomatoes, which benefit from high levels of soil nutrition. Other fruit may only need a mulch of compost every few years. The same applies to most annuals.

As a mulch

Compost works well as a mulch. Added to damp soil, it will conserve moisture by limiting evaporation, meaning there is less need to water plants in dry weather.

By cutting out sunlight, compost also serves to suppress weeds. If your compost contains a few weed seeds itself, as it may well do, any weeds growing in it can easily be hoed once they begin to appear.

As growing media

Home-made compost can be combined with other materials to create a variety of growing media: seed compost, plant compost and cuttings compost. These are likely to be materials that you normally buy, and many of them unfortunately make use of peat as their principal component.

By using your own home-made compost and appropriate quantities of other materials like sharp sand, bark chippings, sieved soil and home-made leaf mould (which is described later), you can cut out your own dependence on precious peat and help preserve and conserve the important habitats that peat bogs represent. The National Trust went peat-free in all of its gardens in 2000 and has successfully used alternatives since then.

Peat bogs also absorb and store carbon dioxide. So, by using peat, not only are peat bogs being destroyed but also massive amounts of CO_2 are being released, thus increasing global warming.

WHERE CAN I MAKE COMPOST?

A compost heap is functional and utilitarian and putting it in the place where you can make the best use of it is important. It may not be an object of beauty, but when you consider what it achieves, a compost heap deserves to be well located.

As you'll appreciate by now, a compost heap has two key roles. Firstly it recycles kitchen and garden waste. Secondly it produces garden compost – a valuable material that has a wide variety of uses (as you'll discover later).

So if the compost heap is too far from the kitchen for you to get to it easily, you may be less inclined to use it. Likewise, if it is too far from where you want to use the compost, you may not get into the habit of automatically going to your own supplies of compost.

Compost heaps work best if they are situated on soil, where micro-organisms can move directly into the organic waste and start working their magic.

In the same way the composting process is speeded up if a heap is in direct sunlight; it will work in a shady spot, it just takes a little longer.

How big your heap is will depend on how much material you have to go on it. This is discussed in greater detail later. Compost can be made perfectly satisfactorily in a free-standing heap, provided there is a good mix of material in it. However, using a compost bin (and they come in various shapes and sizes) helps keep it tidy.

WHAT CAN I COMPOST?

Anything that once lived can live again!

Simple, elegantly phrased and practical, this was the message conveyed by John Seymour, who was blazing a trail thirty years ago for the organic, self-sufficient gardener. And composting is an obvious way of bringing about this resurgence of life.

By following a few easy 'dos' and 'don'ts', a variety of organic 'waste' can be recycled in a compost heap. The whole process amounts to a wonderful form of natural alchemy, in which a <u>problem</u> presented by waste is turned into a <u>solution</u> in the form of wholesome, nourishing compost.

At the heart of successful composting is achieving a balance and mix of materials, which is covered later.

For the moment, however, take a look at this list and tick how many of these you have to hand. The availability of some, such as seaweed, bracken or farmyard and stable manure, will be governed by where you live. If you don't have vegetable-eating pets, or you don't drink tea or coffee, then organic waste from these sources won't feature in your compost heap. But there are still plenty of other ingredients that you can productively recycle – as this list shows...

- Bird feathers (use sparingly)
- Bracken
- Coffee grounds
- Comfrey leaves
- Dead flowers
- Dried leaves
- Egg shells
- Farmyard manure
- Fruit skins and cores
- Grass mowings
- Green leaves

- Hair clippings
- Hay (when it is old and spoiled)
- Hutch and cage bedding and manures from pets like rabbits, guinea pigs and hamsters
- Natural fabrics
- Nettles
- Old bedding plants
- Pet hair
- Sawdust
- Scrunched-up cardboard such as toilet roll centres, egg boxes, cereal cartons
- Scrunched-up newspaper
- Seaweed
- Small woody prunings
- Soft hedge clippings
- Soil
- Spent potting compost
- Stable manure
- Straw
- Urine
- Used tea leaves and tea bags
- Vegetable peelings and scraps

- Weeds (perennial weeds should be killed off before being added to the compost heap)
- Windfalls
- Wood ash
- Wool

WHAT CAN'T I COMPOST?

Even items that cannot be composted can usually be recycled at appropriate recycling points, leaving only the minimum quantity of household waste to be sent to landfill.

Among those things that should not be put on the compost heap, some will simply not rot down, others, such as cat and dog faeces, contain dangerous pathogens and some kitchen waste (cooked food, bread, meats, fish and fats) may attract rodents and flies.

Although perennial weeds can be composted once they are dead, putting them directly onto a compost heap after they have been pulled from the soil can be risky. Unless the compost heap reaches a very high temperature, their roots may survive. In fact, some perennial weeds may flourish in the warm moist conditions of a compost heap. So it is probably wisest to isolate the most persistent weeds and allow them to rot down somewhere where they can do no harm. Placing them in a black plastic bin liner is a well-tried method.

These are other items of household waste that should not be put on a compost heap:

- Bulky cardboard boxes (unless broken up and crumpled into smaller pieces)
- Cat litter
- Coal ash
- Cooking grease and oils
- Disposable nappies
- Dog faeces
- Fish
- Foam packaging
- Glass
- Glossy magazines (the finish on the paper they are made from is not suitable for composting)
- Meat
- Metal cans
- Metal foil

- Newspapers (in large quantities)
- Perennial weeds such as bindweed, couch grass, dandelions, docks and ground elder
- Plastic bags
- Plastic containers
- Plastic packaging
- Synthetic fabrics
- Wire
- Woody material (this can take a long time to rot down, so it should be broken up first and may need to be put through several composting cycles before it is usable)

NATURE AT WORK

Left to its own devices nature will recycle organic matter and produce compost. To achieve this, it calls on the services of a host of creatures – worms and microscopic organisms – which rot organic matter by eating it. This happens whether the organic waste falls to the ground or whether it is placed on a compost heap. In a compost heap, the change from waste to compost simply happens more quickly. The reason for this is the supply of nitrogen.

Recycling organic waste into compost requires a lot of nitrogen. When organic waste rots down on the ground the bacteria at work on it draw nitrogen from the soil, which temporarily starves plants growing in the vicinity of the nitrogen they need to thrive.

In a compost heap, nitrogen is added as part of the mix of materials. This enables the bacteria to get to work right away, with a further benefit – they produce a lot of heat in the process. Heat is important in a compost heap and it can be impressive, producing temperatures of up to 66°C. Heat like this will kill the seeds of most weeds and the spores of most plant diseases; it also brings about useful changes in the organic matter itself.

The creatures that work as composters require only three things to keep them active below ground, on the surface and in the compost heap. It doesn't matter where they are, provided that they have air, water and food they will keep eating organic waste and converting it into something that will benefit other plants: compost.

So, as long as they have these three key elements, worms and microscopic organisms can be left to get on with their work, while gardeners get on with theirs.

By using a compost heap, a gardener gives nature a helping hand.

GETTING THE RIGHT MIX

If there is one rule to making compost successfully it is combining a variety of materials. Trying to make compost with too much of one material – grass mowings for example – will not give satisfactory results. Although you may produce more grass mowings than other compostable materials, piling these onto a compost heap without the right balance of other material will only result in a nasty smelly sludge.

Composting materials can be divided into two groups, often referred to as 'greens' and 'browns'. Grass mowings and other young sappy materials are 'greens'. Left to rot down on their own, they produce the unpleasant sludge mentioned above.

To produce compost, 'greens' need to be mixed with drier, tougher materials – the 'browns' – which rot down more slowly. 'Browns' also provide fibre in compost, which gives it a good structure.

It's worth knowing that these 'greens' and 'browns' also represent two important chemicals that are crucial to the composting process. 'Greens' are rich in nitrogen, 'browns' are rich in carbon – and getting a good balance of these lies at the heart of making compost successfully.

The Centre for Alternative Technology (details of which can be found at the end of the book) has devised a very effective analogy for a good compost mix: the cheese sandwich. The two slices of bread in the sandwich represent the 'browns' – the drier, harder materials rich in carbon. The much thinner slice of cheese equates to the 'greens' – soft, wet materials with a high nitrogen content.

The cheese sandwich analogy also shows the relative proportions of 'greens' and 'browns' that produce good compost: basically, you need more 'browns' than 'greens'.

Although there may be a chemical formula for the ideal compost mix, you can get the correct balance of 'greens' and 'browns' by watching what happens to your compost as it rots down.

- **If the compost starts to go wet and sloppy, add more 'browns' (scrunched-up cardboard, for example)**
- **If the compost looks dry, add more garden waste and kitchen scraps <u>and</u> don't forget to water the heap**

Of course, many waste organic materials already have a good mix of 'green' and 'brown' in their own structure, which makes them well-balanced composting material. These include:

- **Bracken**
- **Coffee grounds**
- **Dead flowers**
- **Farmyard manure**
- **Fruit skins and cores**
- **Hutch and cage bedding and manures from pets like rabbits, guinea pigs and hamsters**
- **Nettles**
- **Small woody prunings**
- **Soft hedge clippings**

- Soil
- Spent potting compost
- Stable manure
- Used tea leaves and tea bags
- Vegetable peelings and scraps
- Weeds (perennial weeds should be killed off before being added to the compost heap)
- Windfalls

Quick-rotting 'greens' include:

- Comfrey leaves
- Grass mowings
- Green leaves
- Old bedding plants
- Seaweed

Slow-rotting 'browns' include:

- Dried leaves
- Hay (when it is old and spoiled)
- Natural fabrics
- Old bedding plants
- Sawdust

- Scrunched-up cardboard such as toilet roll centres, egg boxes, cereal cartons
- Scrunched-up newspaper
- Small woody prunings
- Straw
- Wood ash
- Wool

HEAPS, BINS AND BOXES

How you make compost is entirely up to you. You can build a free-standing heap. You can construct a bin or box using timber, bricks, concrete blocks or wire netting, which will keep the heap neat and tidy. You can buy commercially produced, pre-fabricated wooden bins and boxes. Or you can buy a variety of plastic bins – many of which are available from local councils at subsidised prices that encourage home composting (further details about this can be found at the end of the book).

Compost heaps
Although using a bin or box (like those described below) will keep a compost heap neat and tidy, compost can be

produced from simply piling various types of organic material – both 'greens' and 'browns' – in layers.

In order to generate and retain sufficient heat, a free-standing heap needs to have a base measuring at least two metres by a little over a metre. This will taper as it rises. However, it will have a greater surface area through which more heat may be lost than from a more compact heap in a box or bin.

Start by forking over the ground where you plan to put it; this improves drainage and will make it easier for worms and other composting creatures to move upwards into the heap.

The bottom layer should comprise soft twiggy material about 20cm deep. Any unrotted material from another compost heap can form the next layer. Failing that, cover your base layer with a thin layer of soil about five centimetres deep. Then you can add layers of 'greens' and 'browns', remembering to keep a balance. By adding these in layers you can be sure that air and moisture will circulate within the heap.

If the weather is dry, the materials at the sides of the heap can dry out. To keep them moist, pour one or two watering canfuls all around the edge.

If the heap looks soggy, add a greater proportion of 'browns' to balance the moisture content.

Build the heap a little over a metre high with gradually tapering sides and a <u>flat</u> top. Having a flat top is important because it minimises the amount of uncomposted material all around the outer areas. Most of us tend to put material into the centre of a compost heap. However, the centre is best reserved for mushy, sappy material, while firmer materials are placed around the edges to maintain a flat surface at the top of the heap.

Cover it with sacks or old carpet to retain the heat that builds up and let nature do the rest. Hessian sacks are ideal for this purpose and can often be picked up from pet shops.

When the compost is ready to be used, dig into the heap and it will be there waiting for you. Any material on the outside of the heap, which has only partially rotted down, can be mixed into the next heap you make. When it comes to composing compost, nothing goes to waste!

DIY compost box

You can construct perfectly successful compost bins with different kinds of materials. In each case you should construct three walls, with air gaps, around a square measuring no smaller than a metre in both directions. (If there is lots of material available, the box can be bigger.)

On the open side drive two stout posts into the ground, positioned so that each one is in line with one of the open sides and stands a couple of centimetres away from it.

The gap between the two posts and the end of the wall will provide space for wooden slats to be dropped into place to hold the contents of the heap while the compost is forming, When it is ready to be used, the slats can be lifted out to give easy access to the heap. Make sure, though, that an air gap is left between each layer.

You could construct a bin from materials such as...
- **Redundant wooden pallets, insulated with cardboard, paper, straw or hay, held in place by a lining of wire netting.**

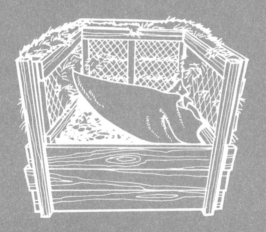

- **Bricks or concrete blocks.**

- **Two layers of wire netting, shaped into three sides of a box by four wooden posts (one at each corner) and insulated with cardboard, paper, straw or hay.**

If you are concerned about rats getting into your compost, the tip given earlier should keep them away – bury wire netting to a depth of 30cm around all outer sides of the compost heap and bring this netting up to the top of the compost box.

Beehive bins

If you are handy with a saw and hammer, you might consider making a layered 'beehive' bin. This consists of horizontal sections made from four wooden boards nailed together. The corners of each layer are reinforced by

wooden battens that stand proud of the upper edge. These hold the sections together securely when one layer is dropped on top of the one below, with space for air to circulate between the layers.

As a compost heap grows, another layer of the 'beehive' box can be added.

In the same way, layers can be removed and used to start a fresh heap, as an existing one shrinks or when the compost is ready to be used.

New Zealand box

You can buy these ready made, or you can construct one yourself. Either way you will end up with what many gardeners regard as the last word in compost bins.

Devised in New Zealand, as its name suggests, this is a wooden structure that has the benefit of providing two (sometimes three) separate compartments – side by side. The front of each individual chamber is fitted with vertical slots into which wooden slats or boards can be dropped, as in the bins described above. And like them, access to the heap is easy in a New Zealand box. Lift out the boards and you can fork or shovel the heap with ease.

If there is enough space in the garden, having three boxes lets you make compost in the easiest way. The heap in the first box is the one that is currently being filled. The second box contains a full heap that is busy 'making' compost. The third box has the heap of compost that is being 'mined' for its humus.

Any uncomposted material in the third box is put into the heap in the first box, to be put through the compost recycling process a second time.

When the first box is filled, it should be covered with carpet or sacking and left to rot down. All the compost in the third box needs to be removed, so that it can be filled with organic waste – in effect, it becomes the next 'box number one'.

Daleks, Dustbins and Tumblers

Inexpensive composters provided by most councils are usually 'Dalek'-type plastic containers. These have removable lids, for filling the container, and some have a door at the bottom for taking out compost once it is made.

An old plastic dustbin can be used in the same way as a 'Dalek' composter. All you need to do is cut out the bottom of the dustbin and turn it upside down, so that you can lift it clear of the compost when it is ready for use.

Compost tumblers are another type of plastic container. Instead of standing stationary on the ground, though, these are mounted on a pivoting frame – as their name suggests, tumblers are designed to be rotated every day. This makes them ideal for dealing with dense, wet, kitchen waste, which can be aerated regularly by the tumbling motion.

Kitchen and garden waste is placed inside the tumbler along with a few handfuls of finished compost or garden soil to get the process started. By rotating the contents of the tumbler every day, it is well aerated and well mixed, leading to successful compost production. Tumblers are also useful for mixing materials before they are put into a stationary compost bin.

Green Cones

Not all composting systems produce compost that you remove to use in other parts of the garden. Green Cones are popular 'digesters' in which organic waste breaks down and is drawn directly into the surrounding soil through the action of worms.

Unlike other composting containers, which sit on the surface, the Green Cone has a basket-shaped base that is buried in the ground. Above this sits the cone, through the top of which waste material is dropped inside. There worms and micro-organisms get to work on it, and continue the process by drawing the composted material they produce down into the ground. Since a lot of kitchen waste has large quantities of moisture, this also seeps into the soil as a rich feed that nearby plants can take up.

Waste digesting units, like Green Cones, require more careful installation than other compost boxes and bins that stand on the surface. Depending on the soil in your garden and how much material goes into your digester, it may require moving to a new location after a year or two, so that another part of the garden can benefit from the material recycled through it.

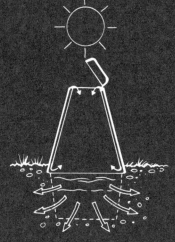

TO TURN OR NOT TO TURN

Some people are put off the idea of making compost by the prospect of having to set to with a fork regularly to turn large amounts of heavy organic material in the compost heap.

For them – and everyone else with similar misgivings – reassurance is at hand. You don't have to turn a heap to make compost. In fact you don't have to touch a compost heap at all apart from adding organic material and using the compost once it is ready.

The downside is that it will take considerably longer for the compost to form if it is left to get on by itself – a good many months and possibly as long as a year. Still, many gardeners are quite happy to leave nature to get on with the recycling in its own time. What's the hurry? they ask. Those who have the space sometimes opt to have several compost bins, so that over time they develop a steady supply of usable compost. While more recent heaps are rotting down, the one that has been decomposing longest is delivering compost to the garden.

So, not turning a compost heap is an acceptable option. You just can't be in a hurry to begin using your compost, if that's what you decide to do.

If you have the energy and inclination to turn your heap, the process of making compost will be noticeably quicker. This is because turning it increases oxygen flow, blends materials and gives you the chance to check on the condition of the heap – whether it has the right level of moisture and whether you need to add water or drier, woodier, 'brown' material to improve the balance of ingredients.

To some gardeners the process of turning a compost heap is akin to secondary fermentation in champagne. It stimulates another heating process, which gets all the micro-organisms working again.

The time to turn a heap is when it starts to cool. By this stage it will have shrunk considerably. If you are using two (or three) compost bins, like the New Zealand boxes mentioned earlier, all you do is fork the material from one bin into the other. If your compost is in a single heap, either in a bin or free-standing, turning involves taking it apart and rebuilding it. In both cases it's important that the material on the outer edges of the original heap goes into the centre of the rebuilt one, where it will be exposed to the greatest heat and micro-organic activity.

As you'll discover in a moment, time and effort spent turning a heap regularly is rewarded by rapidly produced compost. This amount of work isn't for everyone and it doesn't matter that it isn't. Everyone who makes compost will get it in their own time. Those who opt for turning, just get it quicker.

Whether you decide to turn or not to turn, the end product will be the same. When you can no longer recognise most of the original material that went into the heap, your compost will be ready to use. Don't worry about the odd piece of egg shell, or stubborn woody strand. While it's true that leaving it longer will produce finer compost, if most of the original contents have decomposed satisfactorily, you can use what the worms and other composting creatures have provided you with.

Remember too, that any material that hasn't fully decomposed can be used to start the next heap you build.

ALL TOGETHER NOW
– TURNING UP THE HEAT

If you have a large quantity of mixed organic waste material, you can build a compost heap in one go. Well mixed and well insulated, a complete compost heap built in a single session can get impressively hot within a few days.

(Making use of a large quantity of material at one go is also the quickest way to produce compost, though it only suits people who have access to enough varied organic waste at one time.)

If you have a shredder, this is ideal for chopping up the chunkier, woodier 'brown' material. But a shredder isn't essential; chopping it up with a sharp spade will do just as well.

Before you start making the heap, mix all the ingredients thoroughly.

Your aim should be to fill whatever bin or container you are using. The best time to do this is at the peak of the growing season, when there is plenty of plant material.

But before you start adding material, fork over the ground where you are going to build the heap. This will help surplus moisture drain away and will help worms and other composters in the soil work their way into the heap of organic material you are laying on for them.

Pile the material, building it in layers about 20–30cm (8–12in) high. As each layer is completed, press it down gently and water it if it is dry.

Add the next layer and repeat the pressing and watering until the heap is complete. It will soon shrink, so you can afford to pile material above the top of the bin or box you are using.

Keeping the heat inside is important when compost is being made quickly in this way, so be sure to insulate it well with carpet or sacking.

The heap will soon begin to heat up. Keen compost makers keep a watch on the temperature by probing the interior of their heaps with thermometers and when you remove the insulating cover on the top, you should be able to see steam rising from the heap.

When the temperature starts to drop, the heap will need turning. (To make compost quickly in this way, you have to turn it.)

To emphasise what was said earlier:
- Turning lets you mix all the materials, moving those that were on the outside into the middle and vice versa.
- Turning also lets you check on the moisture level in the heap. If it is too wet, remix it adding more 'brown' material to absorb the surplus moisture. If the heap appears to be too dry, you could either water it or add more 'green' sappy material.

You should notice the heat in the heap picking up again after turning. When this begins to drop, repeat the turning process described above and keep turning it as often as you can. Your efforts will be repaid before long by a supply of rich, ready-to-use compost.

By 'cooking' compost in this way, it can be ready for use in as little as 12 weeks in summer.

A LITTLE AND OFTEN

In households where kitchen and garden waste is available in dribs and drabs it isn't practical to build an entire compost heap in one go. But this doesn't matter. It may take longer, but you can make compost just as well by adding material to your heap when it is available.

The same principles of having a mix of materials still apply to a heap that is accumulated bit by bit. If you have a predominance of kitchen scraps, weeds and grass mowings, you can balance this 'green' material with scrunched-up waste paper and cardboard, 'brown' material, which will add body to the heap and also enable air to circulate in it.

Making compost in this way couldn't be simpler. You just add organic waste to your heap when you want to dispose of it and leave the composting creatures from the soil to get on with their work. As the material rots down and decays, it shrinks and you may find that you never fill the compost bin to the top. Don't worry about it – compost will still be forming.

To see how things are going, look inside the heap a couple of times a year, either by lifting off the plastic container in which you put your organic waste, or opening the front of the box or bin. Down at the bottom you should find rich, dark, friable compost. Above this will be layers of material in various stages of decay. At the top of the heap, the most recently deposited waste will only just have started to rot down.

To make use of the compost that has formed, separate it from the rest of the heap. Then just pile all the unrotted material back into the heap and leave it to carry on decaying as more material is added above it.

That's all there is to it.

LEAF MOULD

Leaf mould is a rich, dark material that serves as a valuable soil improver and conditioner produced by the rotting down of leaves, most of which fall in autumn. It takes considerably longer for leaf mould to form than for compost to be made from recycled waste – the process is different as well – so most gardeners prefer to make leaf mould in a separate container. Having said that, some fallen leaves can be added to a compost heap to provide a balance to moist kitchen waste and grass mowings. So it can be handy to keep a couple of bags of fallen leaves beside a compost heap to mix with other material now and again.

Most types of leaf can be used to make leaf mould, although evergreen leaves like laurel, holly and conifer needles are best avoided. Leaves with a high tannin content, such as oak and beech leaves, make the best leaf mould.

As it rots down leaf mould never generates the kind of heat found in a compost heap, so it does not need to be as well insulated. A container made from wire or plastic netting is all that is needed to stop the leaves blowing away and keep them secure while they rot down. This can be easily made using four wooden stakes driven into the ground, around which the netting can be secured.

Smaller quantities can be left to decompose in a plastic sack, with a few air holes punctured in the sides and tied loosely at the top.

If you're putting them into a wire netting bin, the leaves can be trodden down until the bin is full. It's best to collect leaves after it has rained, because they take a very long time to rot down if they are dry. As an alternative, you can water them while you fill the bin.

That's pretty much all there is to it – apart from being patient. By the time autumn comes round again and the next fall of leaves is ready to be collected, the previous season's leaf mould will have rotted down to make a useful mulch.

If you leave it for another twelve months, two-year-old leaf mould is a significantly finer material that can be used as a soil improver and beneficial addition to potting mixtures. As well as a good bulking agent, fine leaf mould retains moisture well and is also rich in micro-organisms that combat disease in plants.

Many gardeners remove the wire netting bins to start a new cycle of leaf mould, leaving their original heap to rot down on the ground; or they construct a new bin for the fresh leaves. Once the leaves have decayed for twelve months, there is no chance of them blowing untidily around the garden, so a container is only necessary to keep the leaf mould heap neatly confined. (It's worth remembering that leaves don't have to have rotted down completely before leaf mould can be used for a number of garden purposes.)

Having emphasised the time it takes for leaf mould to form, you can speed up the process by mixing grass mowings with the leaves the following spring, adding about a quarter of the volume of grass to the leaves. This will produce a cross between compost and leaf mould within a year.

Leaf mould can benefit a garden in a number of ways:
- **To improve soil structure, making it more fertile.**
- **As a mulch to retain moisture.**
- **As winter cover on bare soil to protect newly sown seeds.**
- **To repress weeds.**
- **As a top-dressing for lawns when mixed with loam and sand.**

Making leaf mould is another example of how something seen by many as a nuisance in the garden (which is how a fall of autumn leaves is sometimes perceived), can be turned into something enormously beneficial. When you consider that it takes almost as much time and effort to gather leaves and burn them on a bonfire as it does to make leaf mould, it seems an awful waste to put a match to such a useful gardening resource and leave it to smoulder unpleasantly, creating another environmental nuisance.

AT HOME WITH WORMS

Common-or-garden earthworms are invaluable workers in the kind of conventional composting process described so far – one in which quantities of kitchen waste and garden waste decompose together.

However, close relatives of these earthworms – brandling, or tiger worms – specialise in decomposing plant waste, and because of this they can be found in piles of decaying leaves, in manure and in compost heaps.

Leaving normal earthworms to get on with making compost in compost heaps, brandling worms can be housed in specially designed worm bins, or wormeries, to produce worm casts – a particularly rich form of compost.

In households where the main organic material for composting is kitchen waste and vegetable scraps – and where these are only available in relatively small quantities – using a wormery may be the ideal way of recycling waste material.

- It takes up less space than a compost heap.
- Some wormeries can be situated indoors.
- A wormery works with only small quantities of material added at a time.
- Worm compost is richer than garden compost, which makes it a form of home-made concentrated fertiliser.
- As well as compost, wormeries produce a liquid which acts as a rich plant feed when diluted with water.

Wormery designs
Worm bins need several layers in order to work efficiently. This makes them more complex structures than the compost bins and boxes described earlier.

Instructions on how to make DIY wormeries can be found on various websites and in books. A plastic dustbin is a popular choice. This will need drainage holes near the base to allow surplus liquid to seep away. There should also be a layer of gravel in the bottom with a circular wooden board sitting on top of it. The board needs to fit the diameter of the dustbin to prevent the worms from dropping into the drainage reservoir – and a few small holes drilled through the board will allow liquid to percolate out of the material above into the reservoir below.

It's important to isolate the worms from the liquid as it builds up. If you don't the worms may drown.

With the gravel and protective board in place, the worm bin is ready for use.

It is also possible to buy commercially produced worm bins, many of which are designed as a series of easy-to-use stacking sections that separate different layers of material in the wormery. A lot of commercial worm bins are supplied with 'starter kits' containing everything you need to get going – including the most important component of every wormery, the worms themselves.

Working up to full production

If you buy your wormery as a kit, instructions on how to set it up and how to use it will be supplied. If you construct your own wormery, you can still buy your worms by mail order. Either way, your worms will need a good layer of damp bedding material, such as:

- Torn-up newspaper
- Shredded cardboard
- Leaf mould
- Compost
- Well-rotted sawdust
- Any combination of these

The one thing the bedding layer should <u>not</u> be made from is raw, uncomposted material of any sort.

Once your wormery is ready you can order your worms. You should aim to begin with about 1000 worms (about 500g [1lb] in weight). Using a smaller number means that the process will take longer to get started.

Leave the worms to feed on the bedding layer for a couple of days while they settle in.

When you introduce your kitchen and vegetable waste, only put in small amounts at a time. Worms may be able to eat approaching their own weight of food in a day, but they don't appreciate having a large quantity dumped on them. Apart from anything else, a large mass of waste may well start to compost and generate heat, which the worms will not appreciate.

The kind of household waste that <u>can</u> be put into a wormery includes:
- Coffee grounds
- Egg boxes

- **Egg shells**
- **Fruit peelings**
- **Kitchen paper**
- **Paper bags**
- **Shredded cardboard**
- **Shredded paper**
- **Tea bags**
- **Tea leaves**
- **Vegetable peelings**
- **Vegetable stalks**

Household waste that should <u>not</u> be put into a wormery includes:

- **Cat litter**
- **Citrus peel**
- **Dairy products**
- **Dog faeces**
- **Fish**
- **Glass**
- **Meat**
- **Plastic**
- **Tins**

The best idea is to begin by putting small quantities of material into the wormery and watching how the worms get on. As they increase in number and you get a feel for how much they can comfortably consume, you can increase the quantities accordingly. But be careful not to get carried away and load in more than the worms can manage. They will be able to survive for several weeks without any new deposits of food.

The quantity of waste processed in a wormery depends on how many worms there are to work away at it and in what temperature they are working. As the worms breed, their numbers will increase rapidly. It may take a year for a wormery to reach full production, by which time the original 1000 worms could have increased fifteen- or twenty-fold.

Worms at work

It's not a bad idea to regard the worms in a wormery as livestock. They don't require much maintenance, but to work efficiently they need the right environment in which to thrive and they need regular feeding.

Worms are sensitive to temperature and they work more slowly in very cold temperatures. The ideal conditions for a wormery are in a temperature range between 12° and 25°C. Wormeries should be kept away from direct sunlight, which can cause them to dry out and the worms to die. If you can find somewhere where the temperatures do not vary too much, this will suit the worms well.

Do remember, though, that a wormery is a domestic appliance. It's there to be used. So make sure that it can be reached easily and efficiently from the kitchen. In that way you will get into the habit of putting aside your kitchen waste and vegetable scraps to be fed to the worms, rather than opening the kitchen bin and slipping them in there to be sent off to landfill by way of your dustbin.

Some gardeners bring their wormeries into a shed for the winter, or insulate them from the cold if they are staying outside. If you have a worm bin with a drainage sump from which the liquid plant feed can be collected, the wormery can be moved into a garage or porch for the winter. Otherwise, it will need to remain outside, where the surplus liquid can drain into the surrounding soil.

Troubleshooting

When it comes to feeding these particular livestock, 'a little and often' should be your motto. Give them more than they can comfortably consume and the organic waste will start to go off before the worms have had a chance to deal with it. The result may be a nasty smell.

Smell is a good benchmark to indicate whether or not a wormery is working as it should. When it's working correctly there should be no smell coming from it. If you do detect a smell, it means that the worms aren't able to consume and process the waste you are giving them quickly enough.

This may be because:
- **More waste has been put into the wormery than the worms can manage.** So, cut back on what you are putting in until the number of worms increases and they can cope with what they are being fed.
- **There is too much fluid in the worm bin.** Either drain off liquid from the bottom of the bin (and keep it to be used as described below). Or, check that the liquid can drain freely into the surrounding soil. Then reduce the

moisture content in the material the worms are working on by adding material that will absorb the surplus liquid: shredded newspaper, egg boxes, paper towels, scrunched-up cardboard. Check that you are not adding excess liquid with future deposits of waste; the moisture in the kitchen and vegetable waste will provide all that the wormery requires.

- **The temperature in the wormery is wrong: either too hot, or too cold.** Move it to a better location, or insulate it.

Harvesting wormery liquid

With the high moisture content of vegetable waste and much kitchen waste, liquid will build up in a wormery. This needs to be drained away before it poses a risk to the worms. As mentioned earlier, some commercially available bins are fitted with a sump in which this liquid can collect and from which it can be drained through a tap.

Straight from the wormery, this is too rich to be used on its own as a plant feed. You should dilute it using ten parts water to one part wormery liquid, when it makes a useful liquid feed, especially for fruit.

Alternatively, the liquid can be watered over a compost heap, to provide nourishment to the creatures at work there.

Harvesting wormery compost

The rich, dark worm-cast compost produced in a wormery will become available after a few months.

Worm bins with stacking layers that can be lifted out make extracting the finished compost easy – you just remove the upper sections and then take out the one containing the finished worm casts. Empty the rich, dark compost into another container, replace the collecting section in the worm bin and then return the other layers in the order in which you removed them.

Getting at the compost in other types of worm bin requires scooping out the top layer of partially decomposed food and worms and putting it carefully to one side, so that it can been replaced when the compost has been removed. With the worms safely out of the way, the compost can be taken out. Then the uncomposted waste and worms can be returned to the worm bin, where they will carry on their work.

Removing worms from their compost

If the compost you take from the worm bin is full of worms, you'll want to separate them and return the worms to the bin before you use the compost.

Choose a dry sunny day and spread the compost over a hard surface to a depth of 5cm. Moisten several sheets of newspaper and lay these over the compost layer, covering up to half of it.

After several hours, the worms will have migrated from the uncovered compost, to shelter beneath the portion covered by the damp newspaper.

Shovel up the uncovered (and by now worm-free) compost, and repeat the process until the worms have been removed from the compost and returned to the worm bin.

Using worm-cast compost

A small amount of worm casts go a long way and it's best to think of this rich material as a fertiliser rather than as compost pure and simple.

With that in mind, you can use it in a variety of ways:

- As a top-dressing for house plants and patio pots.
- As part of a potting mix in hanging baskets.
- As a rich feed during the growing season for hungry feeders like marrows and other fruiting vegetable crops.

LOOKING AT THE
BIGGER PICTURE

You'll appreciate by now that the main focus of this book is on household composting. However, there is a growing movement promoted by central and local government agencies to encourage composting on a community-wide basis.

These take different forms, from centralised composting facilities that handle large quantities of organic household waste gathered as part of the local refuse collection service, to smaller schemes involving a group of allotment holders, for example, who pool their resources, tools, time and talents to make compost that everyone can use and benefit from.

Your local council will be able to provide up-to-date information about what facilities are available where you

live and what assistance can be provided to anyone
wanting to start composting.

There are also a number of very informative websites that
supply similar information on a national scale.

You can find details of these among the sources of further
information that follow.

FURTHER INFORMATION

Centre for Alternative Technology: offers 'solutions to some of the most serious challenges facing our planet and the human race, such as climate change, pollution and the waste of precious resources'.
Centre for Alternative Technology
Machynlleth
Powys   SY20 9AZ
Website/email: www.cat.org.uk
Tel: 01654 705950
Fax: 01654 702782

The Composting Association: a membership organisation, which also supplies technical assistance to non-members.
The Composting Association
Tithe Barn Road
Wellingborough
Northamptonshire   NN8 1DH
Website: www.compost.org.uk
Tel: 0870 160 3270
Fax: 0870 160 3280

Community Composting Network: a membership organisation, which 'supports and promotes the community management and use of waste bio-degradable resources'.
Community Composting Network
67 Alexandra Rd
Sheffield   S2 3EE
Website: www.communitycompost.org
Email: info@communitycompost.org
Tel: 0114 258 0483 or 0114 255 3720

Department for Environment, Food and Rural Affairs: provides advice
and up-to-date information on all these matters.
DEFRA
Customer Contact Unit
Eastbury House
30–34 Albert Embankment
London   SE1 7TL
Website: www.defra.gov.uk
Email: helpline@defra.gsi.gov.uk
Tel: 08459 33 55 77

HDRA: the national charity for organic gardening.
Garden Organic
Garden Organic Ryton
Coventry
Warwickshire   CV8 3LG
Website: www.gardenorganic.org
Email: enquiry@gardenorganic.org.uk
Tel: 024 7630 3517
Fax: 024 7663 9229

National Trust: source of information on what 'green' and composting
initiatives are being run across England, Wales and Northern Ireland at
its historic properties.
The National Trust
PO Box 39
Warrington   WA5 7WD
Website: www.nationaltrust.org.uk
Email: enquiries@thenationaltrust.org.uk
Tel: 0870 458 4000
Fax: 0870 609 0345

Recyclenow: national recycling campaign for England providing practical advice, encouragement and ideas aimed at getting 'more of us to recycle more things, more often and to understand the positive benefits of our actions'.
Website/email: www.recyclenow.com
Tel: 0845 331 3131

Waste Watch: 'a leading environmental organisation working to change the way people use the world's natural resources'.
Waste Watch
56–64 Leonard Street
London   EC2A 4LT
Website: www.wastewatch.org.uk
Email: info@wastewatch.org.uk
Tel: 020 7549 0300
Fax: 020 7549 0301

Waste and Resources Action Programme (WRAP): 'works in partnership to encourage and enable businesses and consumers to be more efficient in their use of materials and recycle more things more often'.
WRAP
The Old Academy
21 Horse Fair
Banbury   OX16 0AH
Website/email: www.wrap.org.uk
Email: info@wrap.org.uk
Tel (switchboard): 01295 819 900
Tel (helpline): 0808 100 2040